My First Pocket Guide

Mississippi

By Carole Marsh

The Mississippi Experience

The GALLOPADE GANG

Carole Marsh
Bob Longmeyer
Chad Beard
Cecil Anderson
Steven Saint-Laurent
Karin Petersen
Billie Walburn
Doug Boston
Jill Sanders
William Nesbitt, Jr.
Kathy Zimmer
Wanda Coats
Terry Briggs
Jackie Clayton
Pam Dufresne
Cranston Davenport
Lisa Stanley
Antoinette Miller
Victoria DeJoy

Published by GALLOPADE INTERNATIONAL

www.mississippiexperience.com
800-536-2GET • www.gallopade.com

Gallopade is proud to be a member of these educational organizations and associations:

NSSEA

ASCD

SHOPA MEMBER™
School, Home, & Office Products Association

Other Mississippi Experience Products

- The Mississippi Experience!
- The BIG Mississippi Reproducible Activity Book
- The Mississippi Coloring Book
- My First Book About Mississippi!
- Mississippi "Jography": A Fun Run Through Our State
- Mississippi Jeopardy!: Answers and Questions About Our State
- The Mississippi Experience! Sticker Pack
- The Mississippi Experience! Poster/Map
- Discover Mississippi CD-ROM
- Mississippi "Geo" Bingo Game
- Mississippi "Histo" Bingo Game

A Word From the Author... (okay, a few words)...

Hi!

Here's your own handy pocket guide about the great state of Mississippi! It really will fit in a pocket—I tested it. And it really will be useful when you want to know a fact you forgot, to bone up for a test, or when your teacher says, "I wonder . . ." and you have the answer—instantly! Wow, I'm impressed!

Get smart, have fun!

Carole Marsh

Mississippi Basics explores your state's symbols and their special meanings!

Mississippi Geography digs up the what's where in your state!

Mississippi History is like traveling through time to some of your state's great moments!

Mississippi People introduces you to famous personalities and your next-door neighbors!

Mississippi Places shows you where you might enjoy your next family vacation!

Mississippi Nature - no preservatives here, just what Mother Nature gave to Mississippi!

All the real fun stuff that we just HAD to save for its own section!

Mississippi Basics

Mississippi Geography

Mississippi History

Mississippi People

Mississippi Places

Mississippi Nature

Mississippi Miscellany

Who Named You?

Mississippi's official state name is...

Mississippi

Word Definition

OFFICIAL: appointed, authorized, or approved by a government or organization

Statehood: December 10, 1817

Mississippi was the 20th state to join the United States.

What's in a Name?

Mississippi gets its name from the Ojibwa (Chippewa) Indians. They called the big river nearby *mici zibi*, which means "gathering in of all the waters." The Choctaws' name for the river was *mish sha sippukrie*, which means "father of waters," or "beyond age." *Messipi* was what it was called by the Algonquins. This means, simply, "big river."

Who are you calling names?

State Nicknames

Mississippi is not the only name by which our state is recognized. Like many other states, Mississippi has an official nickname.

The Magnolia State

The Magnolia is a common tree in the South. It has flowers with large, waxy white petals that have a sweet-smelling aroma. The Magnolia is also the state tree.

State Capital:

Jackson

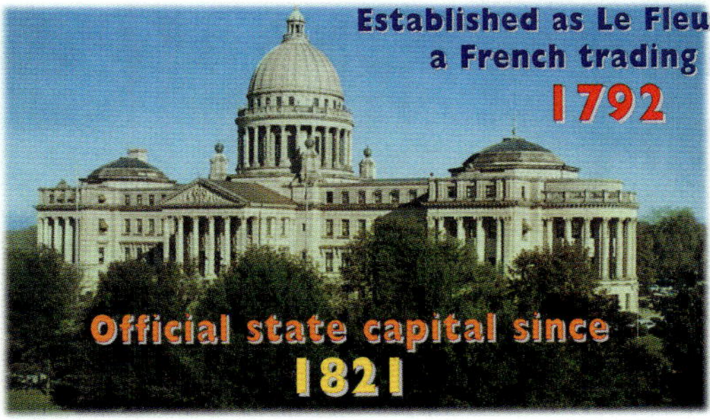

Natchez was named capital of the U.S. Territory of Mississippi in 1798, and in 1821 it was moved to the more central location of Jackson.

Jackson was named in honor of Major General Andrew Jackson, who was the hero of the War of 1812's Battle of New Orleans.

During the Civil War, the city of Jackson was invaded by the Union Army. It was burned in 1863 under orders from Union General William T. Sherman. All that remained were burned-out ruins, and the city was nicknamed Chimneyville.

The governor of Mississippi lives in a mansion that was modeled after the White House in Washington, D.C. It was completed in 1841 and served as the headquarters for General Sherman in 1863.

The state capitol was built in 1903. It is topped by a large dome that rises 180 feet (55 meters) from the ground! The dome is topped by a copper eagle covered with gold leaf. The eagle is 8 feet (2.4 meters) tall and has a wingspan of 15 feet (4.5 meters).

Word Definition

CAPITAL: a town or city that is the official seat of government

CAPITOL: the building in which the government officials meet

Who's in Charge Here?

Mississippi's GOVERNMENT has three branches:

LEGISLATIVE	EXECUTIVE	JUDICIAL
The legislative branch is called the General Assembly.		
Two Houses The Senate (52 members) The House of Representatives (122 members)	The governor, lieutenant governor, attorney general, secretary of state, and seven other officers	Supreme Court (nine justices), followed by Chancery and Circuit Courts, and County, Municipal, Justice and Family Courts

The three branches of government have specific powers and responsibilities to keep one another in check and make sure that a balance of power is maintained.

State Flag

Mississippi's state flag was adopted on February 7, 1894.

The Confederate flag is included in the top left corner to show that Mississippi belonged to the Confederacy during the Civil War. The remainder of the flag is three bars in the national colors of red, white, and blue. The past few years have brought controversy over the Confederate flag and items featuring that symbol.

State Seal

The state seal was adopted in 1817. It features an eagle with outstretched wings. The eagle's breast is covered by a shield bearing 13 stars over vertical stripes. The eagle holds a bundle of arrows in one talon and a palm branch in the other.

Word Definition

MOTTO: a sentence, phrase, or word expressing the spirit or purpose of an organization or group

State Motto

Mississippi's state motto is...

By valor and arms

Mississippi's state motto comes from the Latin, *Virtute et armis.*

Birds of a Feather

The state bird of Mississippi is the Mockingbird, *Mimus polyglottos*. It copies the songs of other birds. Mockingbirds can also copy other sounds such as a dinner bell.

The Mockingbird was adopted in 1944 by the state legislature to be the official state bird after the Women's Federated Club requested it.

Magnolia

Generations pass while some trees stand.

—Sir Thomas Browne

Magnolia trees can grow very tall. Some are as tall as 100 feet (30 meters). They also grow very slowly. This tree was officially designated the state tree on April 1, 1938.

The Magnolia's leaves are large and have a shiny dark green color. They feel almost leathery.

The Magnolia's bloom is a large, white, sweet-smelling blossom.

Magnolia Blossom

Mississippi school children selected the Magnolia Blossom as the state flower in 1900. The legislature made their selection official in 1952.

...Under the blossom
that hangs on the bough.
—Shakespeare

The Magnolia's Latin name is *Magnolia grandiflora*. "Grandiflora" translates into "large flower." The Magnolia Blossom can be 6 to 8 inches (15 to 20 centimeters) across!

White-tailed Deer

White-tailed Deer are so named because when they are frightened and run, their tails stand straight up, and the white underside can be seen. Their tails are almost a foot long (0.3 meter)!

RIDDLE: What do you get when you cross the Mississippi state animal with the state tree?

ANSWER: A deer that grows slowly and can reach 100 feet (30.3 meters) tall, or a tall tree with sweet-smelling flowers that runs fast when it is frightened!

Wood Duck

State Waterfowl

In 1974, the state legislature named the Wood Duck the state waterfowl. These birds are common to the lakes and ponds of Mississippi.

Male Wood Ducks are very colorful with purple, burgundy, navy, and deep green feathers. However, during the summer, their feathers dull, and they look more like the female.

Petrified Wood

Petrified Wood that dates back 36 million years can be found in the Petrified Forest in Madison County. This is the only petrified forest east of the Rocky Mountains. A prehistoric river carried the trees and deposited them in the state's fine sand and silt.

State Fossil & State Shell

Zeuglodon

– *Zygorhiza kochii* –

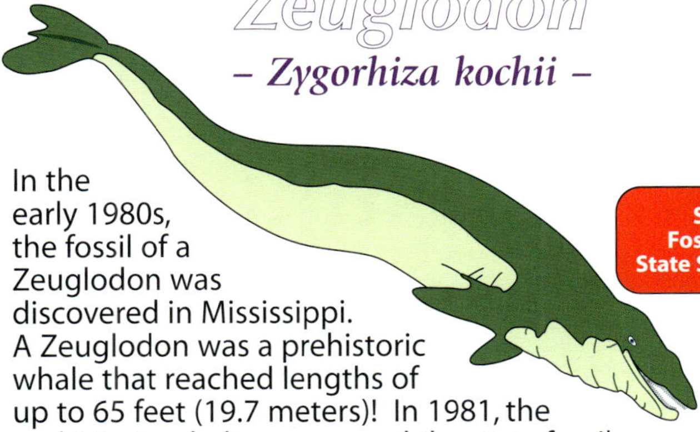

In the early 1980s, the fossil of a Zeuglodon was discovered in Mississippi. A Zeuglodon was a prehistoric whale that reached lengths of up to 65 feet (19.7 meters)! In 1981, the prehistoric whale was named the state fossil.

Oyster Shell

The southern coast of Mississippi is the perfect environment for Oysters. Because they are so abundant there, the Oyster Shell was named Mississippi's state shell.

Bottlenose Dolphin

State Water Mammal

Mississippi's warm coastal waters are home to the Bottlenose Dolphin. These friendly, playful creatures often jump and splash beside ships as they leave the state's ports. Dolphins are favorite performers at many aquariums and water-theme parks. At one time, Dolphins were hunted for their hides and oil.

The Bottlenose Dolphin is actually more common than the common dolphin!

Honeybee

– *Apis mellifera*

Honeybees are important to Mississippi's profitable agricultural economy. Without them, some plants could not produce fruit, which means that they could not produce seeds. After awhile, these plants would die out.

Honey is also an important product to the state. Beekeepers sell the honey produced by their beehives.

Largemouth Bass

—*Micropterus salmoides*—

The Largemouth Bass is a greenish fish with a dark side stripe that lives in Mississippi's quiet, vegetated lakes, ponds, and rivers.

People who fish like to catch Bass because they put up a fight and make catching them a challenge. Largemouth Bass can also grow fairly large—up to 22 pounds (10 kilograms).

Mississippi Bass

Put a bass fillet on foil. Drizzle with lemon juice. Sprinkle with salt and pepper. Add shredded smoked ham and broil fish until done.

In 1813, the Mississippi Territory included all of present-day Mississippi and Alabama. In 1817, Congress divided it into the state of Mississippi and the Alabama Territory.

State Location

Mississippi is in the Deep South. Because of its closeness to the Mississippi River, the area that would eventually become the state was easily reached by European explorers.

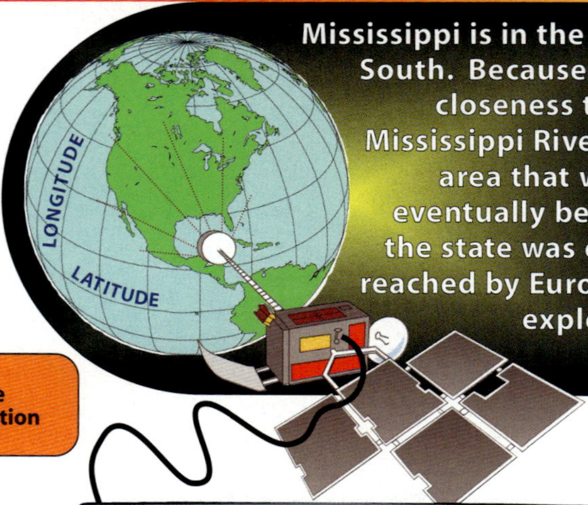

State Location

Word Definition

LATITUDE: Imaginary lines which run horizontally east and west around the globe
LONGITUDE: Imaginary lines which run vertically north and south around the globe

On The Border!

These border Mississippi:

States: Louisiana, Arkansas, Tennessee, Alabama

Bodies of water: Mississippi River, Gulf of Mexico, Tennessee River

I'll Take the Low Road...

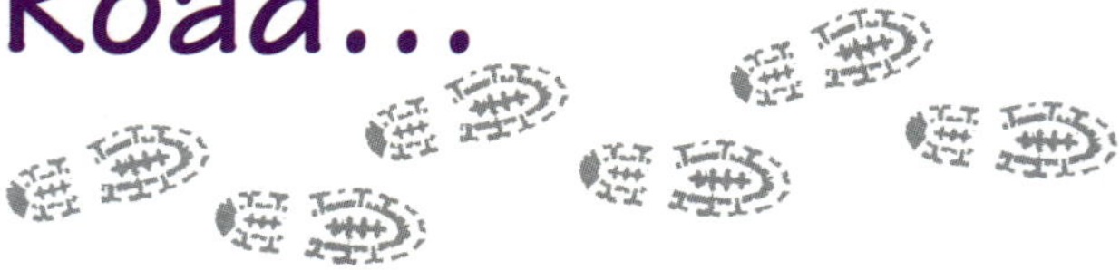

Mississippi is 180 miles (290 kilometers) from east to west...or west to east. Either way, it's a long drive!

Total Area: Approx. 48,266 square miles (125,000 square kilometers)

Land Area: Approx. 46,914 square miles (121,498 square kilometers)

Mississippi is 330 miles (530 kilometers) from north to south...or south to north. Either way, it's still a long drive!

You Take the High Road!

Highest Point

Woodall Mountain is 806 feet (246 meters) tall and is the highest point in Mississippi. It is located in the northeastern part of the state near the Alabama border and the Tennessee River.

The average elevation in Mississippi is 300 feet (90 meters) above sea level!

Lowest Point

Sea level—along the Gulf of Mexico

I'm County-ing on You!

Mississippi is divided into 82 counties.

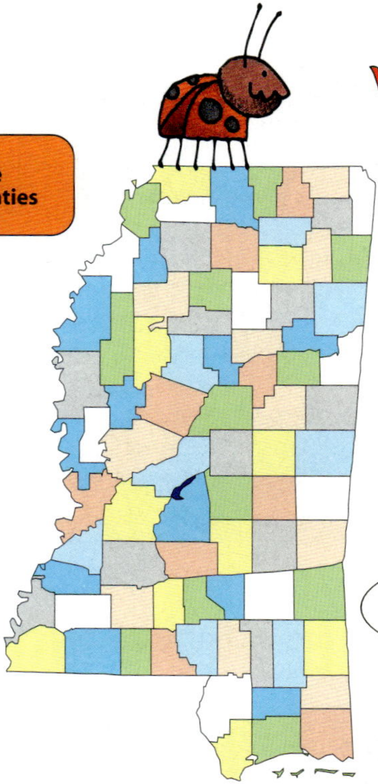

Word Definition

COUNTY: an administrative subdivision of a state or territory

It's All Natural!

Mississippi has more tree farms than any other state. In all there are more than 5,700 tree farms. The state also produces a wide variety of trees numbering more than 120 varieties.

Word Definition

NATURAL RESOURCES: things that exist in or are formed by nature

Minerals and rocks:

- Limestone
- Sand
- Gravel
- Clay—including bentonite, fuller's earth, ball clay, kaolin, and clays for bricks and tiles

Petroleum and natural gas are also found in Mississippi, but they are not a big part of the state's economy!

Mississippi's catfish farming industry is the largest in the nation. More than 65 percent of the world supply comes from Mississippi waters.

Weather, Or Not?!

The moist, mild climate of Mississippi makes for long, hot, humid summers and short, temperate winters. Mississippi's hottest month is July when the average temperature is 81°F (27°C). The coldest month is January, with an average temperature of 46°F (8°C). Mississippi gets about 57 inches (145 centimeters) of rain a year.

Highest temperature: 115°F (46°C) at Holly Springs on July 29, 1930

°F=Degrees Fahrenheit — °C=Degrees Celsius

Lowest temperature: -19°F (-28°C) at Corinth on January 30, 1966

Mississippi's warm, moist air often produces violent weather such as hurricanes and tornadoes. Some of the state's tornadoes have produced winds up to 300 miles per hour (483 kilometers per hour).

Topography

Back On Top

The alluvial plain makes up much of Mississippi. In prehistoric times, rivers heading into the Mississippi River would flood and then recede, leaving behind large deposits of rich, fertile soil known as alluvial. Today this plain makes up 35,000 square miles (90,600 square kilometers) of lowland. It is some of the richest farmland in the world.

The Delta is the land between the Mississippi and Yazoo Rivers. It, too, is known for its fertile soil.

Mississippi has sandy coastal regions, and areas filled with piney woods and prairies. The area east of the alluvial plain is one filled with a fine yellow-brown soil called loess.

The most rugged terrain is found in the northeastern part of the state.

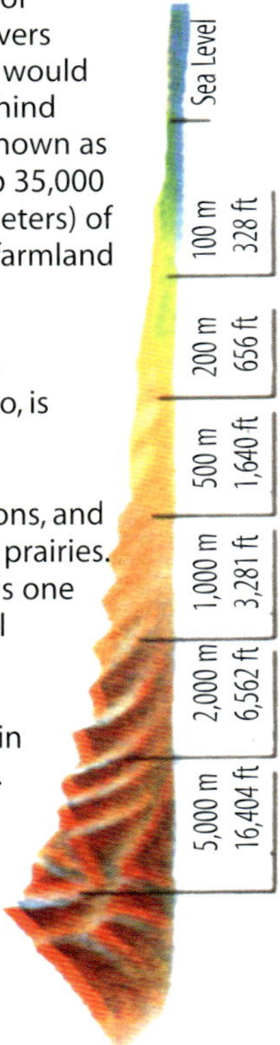

Word Definition

TOPOGRAPHY: the detailed mapping of the features of a small area or district

Mounds Abound!

The first residents of the Mississippi area were probably Indians who migrated there from Asia. People began arriving more than 12,000 years ago. Some of these people built large earthen mounds.

Scientists have tried to figure out exactly why the mounds were built. Some believe they may have been used to escape the mighty river's floodwaters. Some archaeologists have found fences around the mounds, making them think the mounds may have served as forts. Still others think they may have been used for religious purposes. There is even the belief that they were used as platforms for sending signals!

The main mounds in Mississippi are the Lake George Site near Yazoo City, Winterville Mounds north of Greenville, and Emerald Mound near Natchez.

A River Runs Through It!

The Tallahatchie Bridge is mentioned in a ballad that was popular in the 1960s.

Here are some of Mississippi's major rivers:

- The Mississippi, of course!
- Big Black
- Yazoo
- Coldwater
- Sunflower
- Tallahatchie
- Pearl
- Pascagoula
- Tombigbee

Did you notice that a number of Mississippi's rivers have Indian names? How many can you count?

Gone Fishin'

Mississippi has a number of "oxbow" lakes. These crescent-shaped lakes were formed when the Army Corps of Engineers crimped off some of the curving route of the Mississippi and made its course straighter.

OXBOW LAKES

- Lake Beulah
- Lake Lee
- Lake Washington
- Lake Whittington
- Moon Lake
- DeSoto Lake
- Grand Lake

BAYOU: a marshy stream that moves slowly

Word Definition

BAYOUS

- Bayou Pierre
- Bayou Chitto

Word Definition

RESERVOIR: a body of water stored for public use

RESERVOIRS

- Pickwick Lake
- Arkabutla Lake
- Grenada Reservoir
- Enid Reservoir
- Sardis Reservoir
- Ross Barnett Reservoir
- Beulah Lake

ARE YOU A CITY MOUSE... OR COUNTRY MOUSE?

Have you heard of these wonderful Mississippi town, city, or crossroad names? Perhaps you can start your own list!

SMALLER TOWNS:	LARGER TOWNS:
Alligator	Jackson
Basic	Gulfport
Bigpoint	Biloxi
Bobo	Hattiesburg
Chunky	Greenville
Love	
Money	
Midnight	
Onward	
Rolling Fork	
Shivers	

Transportation

Major Interstate Highways

There are more than 70,000 miles (112,651 kilometers) of highways in Mississippi.
I-55, I-20, I-59, I-10

Major Airport

Jackson International

Railroads

Mississippi has 20 freight railroads, and 15 cities with passenger train service.

Seaports

Pascagoula
Vicksburg
Gulfport
Natchez
Greenville

Gulfport and Pascagoula are the Gulf Coast's two major seaports.

Major Waterway

The Gulf Intercoastal Waterway passes through Mississippi. It is part of a 1,065-mile (1,714-kilometer) water route that goes from Texas to Florida.

Timeline

- 800 BC-AD 1000 Early Indian culture thrives
- 1541 Hernando De Soto discovers Mississippi River
- 1699 Pierre Le Moyne, Sieur d' Iberville, founds first settlement
- 1729 Natchez Indians attack Fort Rosalie; French wipe out Natchez tribe in retaliation
- 1763 British win control of Mississippi after defeating French in French and Indian War
- 1763-1779 Great Britain rules Mississippi as part of West Florida
- 1779 Spain takes over West Florida
- 1795 U.S. takes over much of West Florida from Spain
- 1798 Congress establishes Mississippi Territory
- 1806 Better variety of cotton seeds arrive from Mexico
- 1811 State's 1st college, Jefferson College, opens
- 1822 Legislature meets in new capital of Jackson
- 1861 Mississippi secedes from Union, joins Confederate states
- 1870 Mississippi rejoins Union; remaining Chickasaw and Choctaw Indians are marched to Oklahoma on "Trail of Tears"
- 1906 Mississippi establishes rural schools
- 1964 Schools integrate; students age 6-13 must go to school
- 1989 Charles Evers elected mayor of Fayette; first black mayor since Reconstruction
- 2001 On to the 21st century!

Here come the humans!

Thousands of years ago, nomadic hunters lived in the area that would one day become the state of Mississippi. They were in search of wild game. The animals they hunted provided food and clothing. These Paleo-Indians were the ancestors of Mississippi's Native American population.

The earliest Mississippians built mounds made of earth. Archaeologists have discovered tools, masks, clay pots, and engraved seashells buried in many of these mounds.

Native Americans Once Ruled!

Mississippi's early Indians soon organized into tribal territories. Three major Indian tribes ruled. The Chickasaws lived in the northern part of the state, the Choctaws in the central part, and the Natchez along the Mississippi River in the southwest.

When the Spanish explorer, Hernando De Soto arrived in 1540, there were between 25,000 to 35,000 Indians living in the Mississippi area.

Word Definition

WAMPUM: beads, pierced and strung, used by Indians as money, or for ornaments or ceremonies.

Land Ho!

The Spanish were the first Europeans to explore Mississippi. In 1541, Hernando De Soto led an expedition in search of gold. Although they never found gold, they did discover the mighty Mississippi River.

The French came next. A group of seven explorers led by Jesuit priest Father Jacques Marquette and Louis Jolliet, a fur trapper, traveled down the Mississippi River from the Great Lakes.

In 1682, René-Robert Cavelier, Sieur de La Salle also came down the Mississippi River from Canada all the way to the Gulf Coast. He claimed the entire area drained by the great river for France and named it Louisiana in honor of the King Louis XIV!

Home, Sweet, Home

Claimed by René-Robert Cavelier Sieur de La Salle, Mississippi now belonged to France. King Louis XIV ordered Pierre Le Moyne, Sieur d'Iberville to occupy the area. In 1699, d'Iberville built the first permanent European settlement, Fort Maurepas, at present-day Ocean Springs. In 1716, Fort Rosalie was established by d'Iberville's brother, Jean Baptiste Le Moyne, Sieur de Bienville, on the site of modern Natchez.

England and Spain were also interested in expanding their territories in the New World. The English had begun trading with the Chickasaw in the late 1600s, and Spain was looking for an opportunity to expand.

By the late 1700s, France, England, and Spain had ruled parts of Mississippi. In 1795, Spain ceded most of the area (now called West Florida) to the U.S. In 1803, the U.S. bought the Louisiana Territory from France, opening the Mississippi River for travel and trade.

King Cotton

For years, cotton was the most important crop in Mississippi. Farmers concentrated on growing cotton. In 1795, Mississippi's first cotton gin was built by a black farmer named Barclay. He based it on Eli Whitney's invention. This helped speed up the process of getting cotton to market. Another boost to "King Cotton" came in the early 1800s when an improved cottonseed from Mexico, called Petit Gulf, made its way into Mississippi.

King Cotton

Cotton made Mississippi one of the richest states in the country when statehood was granted in 1817. In the mid-1800s, no one thought things would ever change. But, cotton depleted the soil in some areas. Then, the Civil War swept through the nation and changed the old ways forever! If things weren't bad enough, in 1907, the boll weevil invaded from the Southwest and destroyed the cotton crop!

Fiddle Facts

During the late 1700s, music and dance were popular among the rough and rowdy Mississippi River rogues of the Natchez Trace—the well-traveled trail between Natchez and Nashville. They especially liked James Gamble, the famous fiddler from Tennessee, who carried his fiddle and bow in a doeskin sack. Once, on his way to a dance, Gamble was attacked by Indians. He managed to save himself and his fiddle. Stuck on his back for several weeks to recuperate, he created a fiddle symphony of the attack, including all the gunfire, screaming, chase, and escape! One popular song from his symphony was "Possum up de Gum Tree."

Natchez-Under-the-Hill was a mile-long (1.6-km) strip of land nestled under the bluffs along the Mississippi River. It was a haven for river rogues.

Freedom!

Once the American colonists were established in their new home, they began to resent the strong-handed rule of royal governors. They objected to paying taxes without representation to a motherland that was no longer their homeland.

Revolution

From 1775 through 1783, during the American Revolution, settlers in southern Mississippi were under British rule and remained loyal to the crown. The northern portion sided with the colony of Georgia and supported the colonists in their struggle for independence.

In 1781, Spain took advantage of Great Britain's involvement in the American Revolution—and, they took control of southern Mississippi. In 1783, Great Britain lost the American Revolution and officially ceded southern Mississippi to Spain.

Of Human Bondage

As a Southern state, Mississippi allowed slavery. Although the majority of landholders did not own slaves, the large plantations and some of the smaller farms depended on slave labor. Slaves brought to America from Africa were forced to grow and harvest tobacco, rice, cotton, and other crops.

Plantation life was one of misery—long days, hard labor, disease, and inclement weather. Slaves were bought and sold and separated from their families whenever their owners chose to do so!

Many slaves shared unique talents, such as creating some of the favorite foods we enjoy today from recipes or seeds they brought from Africa. They also fought for their freedom in creative ways. Slave women created quilts with secret designs to help those wishing to escape find their way along the famous Underground Railroad!

Word Definition

ABOLITIONIST: person who believed slavery was wrong and should be abolished.

The Civil War

Brother

The Civil War was fought over slavery and states' rights. Southern states, with plantations and slaves, were on one side of this conflict. Northern states, who opposed slavery or had no need for it, were on the other side. Some states remained neutral.

On January 9, 1861, Mississippi became the second state to secede (or leave) the Union. A Mississippi resident, Jefferson Davis, was named President of the Confederate States of America. The fighting began in April of 1861 and continued for four long years. More than 3 million Americans fought in the war. As many as 78,000 soldiers were Mississippians.

The Civil War

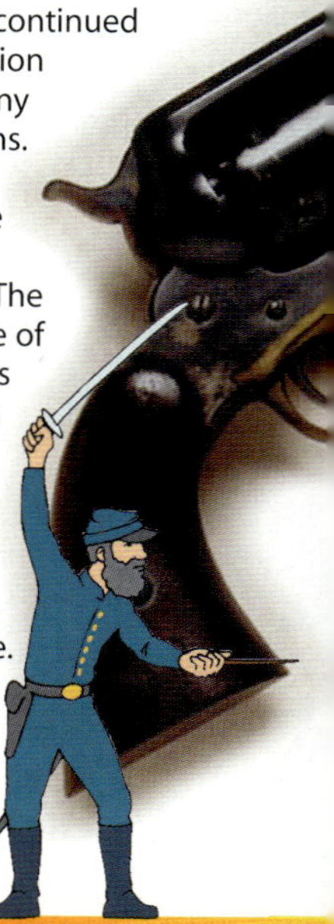

The first battle in Mississippi was the Battle of Shiloh in April 1862. The Confederate troops were defeated. The most important battle was the Battle of Vicksburg in 1863 that lasted 47 days and gave control of the Mississippi River to the Union. General John C. Pemberton surrendered to General Ulysses S. Grant on July 4, 1863. More than 40,000 Confederate and 10,000 Union soldiers died during the siege.

Word Definition

RECONSTRUCTION: the recovery and rebuilding period following the Civil War.

vs. Brother

The Civil War was also called the War Between the States. Soldiers often found themselves fighting against former friends and neighbors, and even brother against brother. Those who did survive often went home without an arm, leg, or both, since amputation was the "cure" for most battlefield wounds. More Americans were killed during the Civil War than during World Wars I and II together!

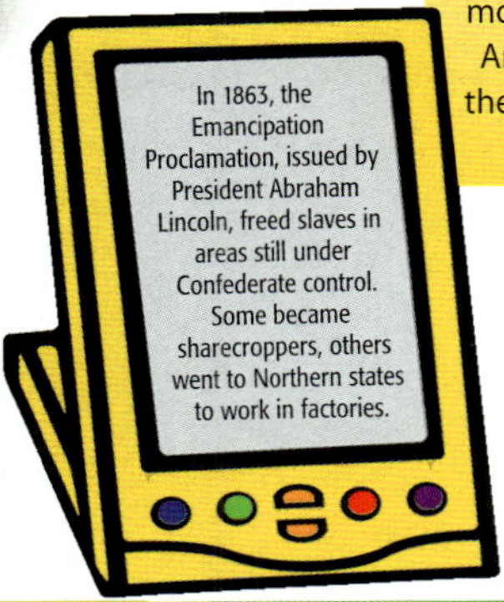

Get It In Writing!

Treaty of Paris, 1783
Established U.S. and Spanish border

State Constitutions
1817, 1869, 1890

Treaty of Dancing Rabbit, 1830
ceded Choctaw land to U.S. Government

Treaty of Pontotoc Creek, 1832
ceded Chickasaw land to U.S. Government which eventually forced all but a few families to relocate in Oklahoma by way of the tragic Trail of Tears

WELCOME TO AMERICA!

Although most Mississippians are native-born, some have come from other states and other countries. As time has gone by, Mississippi's population has grown more diverse. This means that people of different races and from different cultures and ethnic backgrounds have moved to Mississippi. All Mississippians benefit from this diversity!

Immigrants

In the past, immigrants have come to Mississippi from France, England, Canada, West Africa, Italy, and Greece. More recently, people have migrated to Mississippi from Asia and Latin America. Only a certain number of immigrants are allowed to move to America each year. Many of these immigrants eventually become U.S. citizens.

Swoosh!

1840

Tornado tears through Natchez killing 317 people; many of them drown in the Mississippi River.

1893

Hurricane strikes Gulf Coast killing 2,000 people in Mississippi, Louisiana, and Alabama.

1927

Heavy flooding occurs in Delta forcing 200,000 to flee their homes. In 1928, the Flood Control Act requires the U.S. Army Corps of Engineers to control flooding.

1969

Hurricane Camille rips Mississippi coastal cities apart. Ship Island split into two islands! Hundreds of people killed in seven states; more than $1.5 billion in damages!

1890

New state constitution strips African-Americans of their civil rights. A literary test and poll tax, and new residency requirements keep African-Americans from voting.

1936

Governor Hugh White introduces Balance Agriculture With Industry designed to attract new businesses to Mississippi.

1950s & 1960s

Strong civil rights movements occur in Mississippi. Many people persecuted, beaten, and killed.

1965

Voting Rights Act of 1965 helps Mississippi begin to move away from discrimination and violence. The act requires open voter registration for African-Americans. African-Americans allowed to take rightful place in government, schools and universities, and business world!

Women & Children

1884

Mississippi University for Women opens, becoming the nation's first state-supported school for women

1912

Laws pass in Mississippi to regulate child labor

1920

Women gain suffrage nationally through the 19th Amendment

1964

Federal court orders Mississippi's public schools be integrated; children ages 6 to 13 required to attend school

1989

Mississippi's B.E.S.T.–Better Education for Success Tomorrow implemented by Governor Ray Mabus to improve education

Fight!, Fight!, Fight!

Wars that Mississippians participated in:

- War of the Spanish Succession
- French and Indian War
- American Revolution
- War of 1812
- Civil War
- World War I
- World War II
- Korean War
- Vietnam War
- Persian Gulf War

The Mighty Mississippi

The Mississippi River, for which the state is named, is the world's third-longest river. It loops and winds and wiggles its way for 2,348 miles (3,779 km) through our nation—ever changing day by day!

Claim to Fame

In the 1800s, the Mississippi River was America's great highway providing a way for people, household goods, crops, and even farm animals to travel through our young nation. Steamboats, flatboats, pirogues, barges, keelboats, and longboats were a common sight.

Samuel Clemens, better known as author Mark Twain, grew up on the Mississippi River. Many of his beloved stories tell of life on the Mighty Mississippi! Twain even piloted steamboats and traveled along the rough and rowdy Natchez Trace!

The Mississippi River is still America's greatest waterway. The river basin (area drained by the Mississippi and its tributaries) takes up one-third of our nation!

Indian Tribes

Chickasaw • Choctaw • Natchez

These three powerful tribes ruled over many smaller ones including Chakchiuma, Tunica, Taposa, Ibitoupa, Tiou, Ofo, Yazoo, Biloxi, Acolapissa, Pascagoula, and Houma.

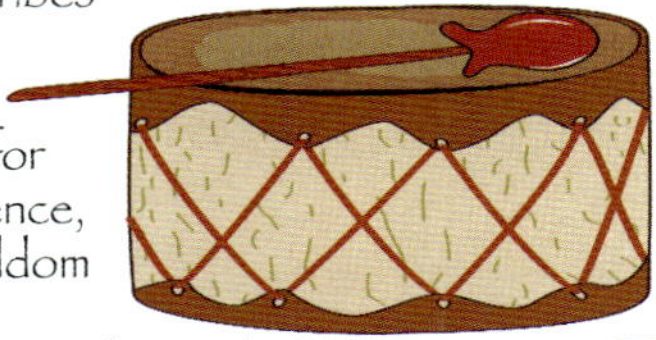

Each of the three major tribes had their own well-established culture. The Chickasaws were known for their strength, independence, and bravery, and were seldom captured. The Choctaw government was a democracy that included a constitution, elections, and courts. A rigid class system existed in the Natchez tribes. The chiefs, who were called Suns, ruled with complete authority over their subjects, the Stinkards.

The Choctaw believed long hair and flat, sloping foreheads to be very special. They achieved this look by pressing boards against the foreheads of male babies soon after birth.

The big chief, the Great Sun, was believed to be descended from the Sun God. Everywhere he went, he was carried on a special litter so his feet didn't even touch the ground!

Here, There, Everywhere!

HERNANDO DE SOTO—Spanish explorer, first European to explore Mississippi

FATHER JACQUES MARQUETTE AND LOUIS JOLLIET—French priest and explorer sailed down the Mississippi River

RENÉ-ROBERT CAVELIER, SIEUR DE LA SALLE—French explorer sailed down the Mississippi River

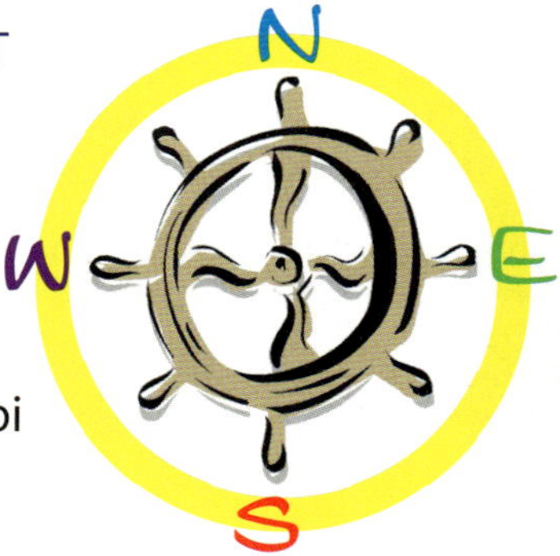

Founding Fathers

These people played especially important roles in early Mississippi!

Pierre Le Moyne, Sieur d'Iberville—was a French explorer who founded the first permanent settlement of Fort Maurepas at present-day Ocean Springs.

Jean Baptiste Le Moyne, Sieur de Bienville—was a French explorer and brother to Pierre. He founded the second settlement of Fort Rosalie at present-day Natchez.

Winthrop Sargent—was the territory's first governor and was appointed by U.S. President John Adams.

Founding Mothers

Varina Howell Davis—was the wife of Confederate President Jefferson Davis.

Paula Ackerman— was the first woman to perform the functions of a rabbi. She was asked to serve after the death of her husband, the acting rabbi, for the Temple Beth Israel congregation.

Rachel Donelson—often took the helm of her father's flatboat so he could shoot at threatening Indians ashore. Rachel eventually became the wife of Andrew Jackson.

Famous African-Americans

Ida Bell Wells—was a daughter of slaves born in Holly Springs. She was a passionate fighter for civil rights and helped found the NAACP (National Association for the Advancement of Colored People).

James Howard Meredith—was the first black student to enroll at the University of Mississippi in Oxford.

Fannie Lou Hamer—fought for the right of blacks to represent Mississippi at the Democratic National Convention in 1964. She worked for educational programs and to improve low-income housing.

Robert Parris Moses—was a student activist who came to Mississippi from Harlem in New York City to work for civil rights. He headed a voter-registration program during the summer known as Freedom Summer.

Blanche K. Bruce—was the editor of the *Floreyville Star*. After the Civil War, he worked for educational programs for blacks. He was the first African-American to serve a full term as a U.S. senator. Bruce also fought against fraud and corruption in federal elections.

Medgar Evers— was a civil rights leader and the head of Mississippi's NAACP. He was killed during the violent 1960s.

DID SOMEONE SAY BOO!?

Confederate Brigadier General William Barksdale was mortally wounded at the Battle of Gettysburg on July 2, 1863, and his body was buried nearby. When his widow, accompanied by the general's favorite hunting dog, came to reclaim the body, the hound began to howl! The body was exhumed and carried away to be buried in Mississippi, but the hound would not abandon the site where his master had been buried. Mrs. Barksdale tried everything she could think of, but the dog remained by the grave. People were touched by the dog's loyalty and put food out for him, but he would not eat. Sadly, he died a few days later. If you are in the area at midnight on July 2, you might hear the mournful cries of the hound guarding his master's grave and awaiting his return!

DO YOU BELIEVE IN GHOSTS?

Sports Figures

JERRY RICE—National Football League (NFL) wide receiver
WALTER PAYTON—NFL running back
ARCHIE MANNING—NFL quarterback
BRETT FAVRE—NFL quarterback
L.C. GREENWOOD—NFL player
WILLIE BROWN—NFL player
JAMES THOMAS "COOL PAPA" BELL—baseball player in the Negro League, ran the bases in 12 seconds or less

JAY HANNA "DIZZY" DEAN—Professional Baseball pitcher
ARCHIE MOORE—professional boxing champion
HENRY ARMSTRONG—professional boxing champion

Many Mississippians have competed and won medals in the Olympics. RALPH BOSTON is Mississippi's most decorated track athlete. In 1984, ROWDY GAINES won a gold medal in swimming. WILLYE B. WHITE is the only female to compete in five consecutive Summer Olympic Games from 1956-1972. RUTHIE BOLTON-HOLIFIELD won Olympic Gold on 1996 and 2000 USA Women's Basketball teams and is a guard for the Sacramento Monarchs Women's professional basketball team.

Entertainers

★ Morgan Freeman—actor

★ James Earl Jones—actor

★ Ray Walston—actor

★ Elvis Presley—rock 'n roll singer and musician, actor

★ Muddy Waters, W.C. Handy, Robert Johnson, and B.B. King—blues musicians

★ Tammy Wynette—First Lady of Country Music

★ Charlie Pride—country music singer

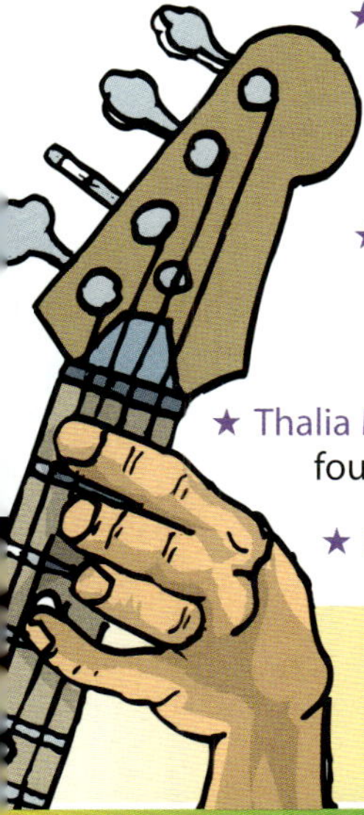

★ LeAnne Rimes—country music singer

★ Leontyne Price and Elen Matos—opera singers

★ William Grant Still—composer, conductor, known as the dean of African-American composers

★ Thalia Mara—professional ballet dancer and founder of the Ballet Mississippi

★ Bob Neill—wildlife writer and raconteur

RIDDLE: Who's known for standing by her man?

ANSWER: Tammy Wynette

Authors

- **William Faulkner**, novelist; works include *The Sound and the Fury*; won Nobel Prize for Literature and two Pulitzer Prizes

- **Eudora Welty**, novelist; works include *The Optimist's Daughter*; awarded Pulitzer Prize for Fiction, Presidential Medal of Freedom and other state, national, and international awards

- **Richard Wright**, novelist who became famous for *Native Son* and *Black Boy*; first African-American author to achieve fortune and fame in the United States

- **Tennessee Williams**, playwright, novelist, poet, writer of short stories; awarded Pulitzer Prize for his play, *Cat on a Hot Tin Roof*. The movie, based on the play, won an Academy Award for Best Picture of 1958.

- **John Grisham**, **Thomas Harris**, and **Greg Iles**, novelists

- **Elizabeth Spencer**, **Walker Percy**, **Willie Morris**, authors

- **Richard Ford**, **Beth Henley**, **Hazel Brannon Smith,** Pulitzer Prize winning authors

- **Hodding Carter**, editor and publisher; received Pulitzer Prize

Word Definition

NOM DE PLUME: French for pen name, a fictitious name a writer chooses to write under instead of his/her real name.

Artists

THEORA HAMBLETT, painter

FLETCHER COX, woodworker

EARL SIMMONS, folk artist

WYATT WATERS, painter

LESLEY SILVER, photographer

MARIE HULL, painter

RICHARD BARTHE, sculptor

George Ohr, the "Mad Potter" of Ocean Springs, was a celebrated potter—but a bit eccentric! Instead of discarding the pots he didn't want to sell, he buried them.

Highwaymen in Mississippi often painted their faces with berry juice and bark stains like Indians on the warpath! Why? To disguise their identity and scare their victims!

Military Leaders

Chief Pushmataha— a Choctaw chief from central Mississippi, fought bravely as a colonel beside General Andrew Jackson in the Battle of New Orleans. He was buried in the Congressional Cemetery in Washington, D.C. with full military honors.

John Anthony Quitman—was a political leader who led volunteer troops in the Mexican War.

General John C. Pemberton—led Confederate troops in the Battle of Vicksburg. He surrendered Vickbsurg to General Grant on July 4, 1863.

Sergeant Henry J. Tudury—was the most decorated soldier of World War I from Mississippi.

General Eleazor Wheelock Ripley—was a hero in the War of 1812. He received the Congressional Medal of Honor.

Colonel William Clark Falkner—served the Confederacy during the Civil War. He was the great-grandfather of William Faulkner (the "u" was added later).

Bernard J. "Bernie" Ebbers— created a long distance discount company called LDDS (Long Distance Discount Service). In 1995, the name was changed to WorldCom and appeared in *Fortune* magazine as one of the largest companies in the U.S. In 1997, WorldCom bought MCI Communications for $37 billion. MCI WorldCom provides local and long distance telecommunications, as well as Internet service, to customers all across the world.

Eliza Jane Pointevent—publisher, was the first woman in the U.S. to publish and own a large metropolitan paper, the New Orleans *Times-Picayune.*

Jim Henson—puppeteer, grew up in Leland and spent lots of time at Deer Creek. The creek and its critters were the inspiration for one of his most famous Muppets–Kermit the Frog. The Jim Henson museum is located on the banks of his beloved Deer Creek.

Oprah Winfrey—First woman to own and produce her own television show, an actress, entertainer, producer, starred in *Beloved*, based on Toni Morrison's novel.

Good Guys: Lucius Quintus Cincinnatus Lamar served in the U.S. Senate after the Civil War. Even though he previously supported withdrawing from the Union, he delivered a heartfelt speech to Congress which helped heal the troubled and torn relationship between the North and South.

Casey Jones was killed in a tragic train accident near Vaughn, Mississippi in 1900. He reached legendary status after a popular folk song was written about him.

Oseola McCarty spent most of her life taking care of other people's clothes–washing and ironing. In 1995, she donated the majority of her lifetime savings–$150,000–to the University of Southern Mississippi in Hattiesburg to create a scholarship for African-American students. Contributions from corporations and individuals have helped the amount of the scholarship grow and grow!

Bad Guys: Joseph Thompson Hare, pickpocket and murderer, had the rare distinction among river rogues of being able to read and write!

Anthony Glass was a merchant, informer, and "fence" who often pointed out wealthy travelers to thieves. After unsuspecting rich folks were robbed, he helped the thieves sell their illegal goods!

The fiercest of all river rogues was called "The cock of the walk."

Political Leaders

JEFFERSON DAVIS–hero in the Mexican-American War, U.S. congressman and senator, president of the Confederate States of America

JOHN R. LYNCH–first African-American from Mississippi elected to the U.S. Congress in 1872

REVEREND HIRAM R. REVELS–first African-American elected to the U.S. Senate in 1870

GREENWOOD LEFLORE–Choctaw chief

JAMES K. VARDAMAN AND THEODORE G. BILBO–governors who supported racial segregation

HUGH WHITE–1930s governor worked to bring new business to Mississippi

JOHN C. STENNIS–U.S. senator

KIRK FORDICE–first Republican governor since Reconstruction

TRENT LOTT–U.S. senator

DAVID HOLMES–first state governor, U.S. senator

ROBERT J. WALKER–U.S. senator, U.S. secretary of the treasury

BELLE KEARNEY–writer, lecturer, state senator

Keeping the Faith

Woodville Baptist Church, Mississippi's oldest church; founded in 1798 and built in 1809

Temple B'nai Israel, Natchez–a 1904 structure standing on the site of the state's first synagogue

First Presbyterian Church, Port Gibson–built in 1859, this church housed a rear gallery for slaves and is known for its unusual steeple decoration of a gold-leafed hand with its index finger pointing heavenward!

Episcopal Church of the Redeemer, Biloxi–Jefferson Davis and his family worshipped here

SCHOOLS

Mississippi has eight private and nine public colleges and universities. Below are a few:

- **Jefferson College**, near Natchez–first college established in the state
- **Mississippi College**, Clinton–founded in 1826; oldest higher education institution still in operation in the state
- **University of Mississippi**, Oxford
- **Mississippi State University**, Starkville
- **Rust College**, Holly Springs–oldest historically black college in the state

Historic Sites

★ **Grand Village of the Natchez Indians**, Natchez–archaeological site

★ **Church Hill**, Springfield–village settled in the late 18th century by a group of Maryland pioneers

★**Vicksburg National Cemetery**–where 17,000 Union soldiers are buried, as well as soldiers from many other wars

★ **Sam Dale State Historic Site**, Daleville–honors General Sam Dale, a frontiersman and hero of the War of 1812

★ **Vicksburg City Cemetery**–burial ground for fallen Confederate soldiers

★ **Nanih Waiya State Historic Site,** east-central Mississippi–Choctaw Indian sacred mound

Parks

★ **Vicksburg National Military Park**–commemorates the siege and defense of Vicksburg; displays the partially restored Union gunboat *Cairo*

★ **Natchez National Historic Park**–centered among one of the country's best-preserved concentrations of homes from the antebellum period

Early Residency

★ **Rosemont Plantation**, Woodville–Jefferson Davis' boyhood home

★ **Weymouth Hall**, Natchez–a raised plantation house overlooking the Mississippi River; built in 1855

★ **Stanton Hall**, Natchez–an 1858 mansion built by Frederick Stanton, who spared no expense on its construction

★ **Longwood**, Natchez–largest and most elaborate octagonal house in the United States; construction was halted in 1861

★ **Shirley House**, Vicksburg–only structure in the Vicksburg National Military Park that survives from the Civil War

★ **Duff Green Mansion**, Vicksburg–built in 1856; a hospital for both Union and Confederate soldiers during the Civil War

★ **Governor's Mansion**, Jackson–built in 1842

★ **Brielmaier House**, Biloxi–built in 1895; this house is now the city's visitor center and beginning of the walking tour of historic buildings

★ **Beauvoir**, Biloxi–post-war home of Confederate president Jefferson Davis

★ **Riverview**, Columbus–an 1850 four-story antebellum house; considered one of Mississippi's finest

Battlefields & Forts

A few of Mississippi's famous Battlefields

- **Brices Cross Roads National Battlefield Site**, west of Baldwyn
- **Tupelo National Battlefield**
- **Vicksburg National Military Park**
- **Battery Robinette**, Corinth

Forts

- **Fort Garrot,** Vicksburg
- **Fort Massachusetts,** West Ship Island
- **Fort Maurepas,** Ocean Springs
- **Old Spanish Fort,** Pascagoula

Sitting atop a 200-foot (60 meters) bluff, Vicksburg was known as the "Gibraltar of the Confederacy."

Libraries

Check out the following special state libraries! (Do you have a library card? Have you worn it out yet?!)

- **Mississippi State Library**
  Jackson–oldest library in the state; established in 1838

- **University of Mississippi Library**
  Oxford

- **Mississippi State University Library**
  Starkville

- **University of Southern Mississippi Library**
  Hattiesburg

Mississippi Attractions

- **J.L. Scott Marine Education Center & Aquarium-Gulf Coast Research Laboratory**, Biloxi
- **Mississippi Petrified Forest**, Flora
- **Jackson Zoological Park**
- **Russell C. Davis Planetarium**, Jackson
- **The Crosby Arboretum**, Picayune
- **Cedar Grove**, Vicksburg–antebellum mansion
- **Cactus Plantation**, Edwards
- **Mississippi Museum of Natural Science**, Jackson

Museums

Maritime and Seafood Industry Museum, Biloxi

Delta Blues Museum, Clarksdale

Mississippi Military Museum, Jackson

Mississippi Museum of Art, Jackson

Casey Jones Museum, Vaughan

Cairo Museum, Vicksburg

Cottonlandia Museum, Greenwood

Turner House Museum, Hattiesburg

Mississippi Agriculture and Forestry Museum, Jackson

Mississippi State Historical Museum, Jackson

Old Spanish Fort and Museum, Pascagoula

- **Biloxi Gulf Coast**, a vacationer's paradise; often called a "museum without walls" because of its colorful 300-year history

- **Waverley Plantation**, Lowndes County, one of the largest plantations in the pre-Civil War South

- **Beauvoir-the Jefferson Davis Shrine**, Biloxi

- **The Old Courthouse Museum–Eva Whitaker Davis Memorial**, Vicksburg

- **Natchez Area**, center of antebellum architecture

- **John C. Stennis Space Center**, near Bay Saint Louis

The Show Must Go On!

International Ballet Competition—Jackson–only three other cities in the world host this prestigious ballet event

The New Stage—Jackson–among the oldest theater groups in the United States

Mississippi Arts Festival—Jackson–held in April; features a wide variety of performing artists

Prairie Arts Festival—Westpoint–held in August

Jubilee Jam–Jackson Arts and Music Fest—held in May

Seashores

The Mississippi Gulf Coast provides wonderful ocean breezes, sandy beaches, floating casinos, swimming, boating, and fishing excursions.

The Gulf Islands National Seashore covers 135,625 acres (54,887 hectares) along the Gulf Coast.

Let There Be Light!

The Biloxi Lighthouse stands in Biloxi Harbor. The lighthouse was built in 1848 and remained in Confederate hands during the Civil War.

Roads...

Natchez Trace Parkway, begins in Tennessee and ends in Mississippi; this road is 492 miles (792 kilometers) long

Hospitality Highway, 32 miles (52 kilometers) long; stretches along the Gulf Coast

Bridges & More!

Saint Louis Bay Bridge

Biloxi Bay Bridge, takes you to the artist community of Ocean Springs

Jamie L. Whitten Bridge, over Tennessee-Tombigbee Waterway

Cypress Swamp Boardwalk Trail, River Bend; winds through the eerie forest of bald cypress and tupelo trees in the Cypress Swamp

Bayous and Deltas

Marshy, slow-moving streams are called bayous. Mississippi bayous can connect lakes with the rivers in the Delta. Others link inland waters with the Gulf of Mexico. Two of Mississippi's bayous are Bayou Pierre and Bayou Chitto.

A delta is a triangle-shaped piece of land formed when sand and soil are deposited at the mouth of a large river. The soil deposits are very rich and fertile. The region between the Mississippi and the Yazoo Rivers is called the Delta. The Delta of Mississippi is often called the "most Southern place on Earth."

Animals of Mississippi

Mississippi animals include:

Alligator
Armadillo
Beaver
Deer
Fox
Muskrat

Nutria
Opossum
Rabbit
Raccoon
Skunk
Squirrel
Terrapin
Weasel

Take A Walk On the Wild Side

Mississippi has a few endangered animals. The white-tailed deer was once among them, but recent efforts to stabilize the population have succeeded and deer are now abundant in the state. Some of Mississippi's endangered animals are:

- Gray bat
- Whooping crane
- Ivory-billed woodpecker

Bison, wolf, and cougar are among the animals that have become extinct in Mississippi since European settlement.

- Barn Owl
- Blue Heron
- Blue Jay
- Bobwhite
- Brown Thrasher
- Cardinal
- Crow
- Dove
- Hawk
- Kingfisher
- Mockingbird
- Pileated Woodpecker
- Seagull
- Warbler
- Wood Duck
- Wood Thrush

Wood Duck

The Mississippi flyway is a main migratory bird route. Migratory birds are found in Mississippi mostly during the winter months. They spend the winter in the warmer Mississippi climate.

Don't let these Mississippi bugs bug you!

Ant
Beetle
Bumblebee
Butterfly
Cicada
Cricket
Dragonfly
Firefly
Grasshopper
Honeybee
Katydid
Praying Mantis
Stick Insect
Ladybug
Mayfly
Moth

Bumblebee

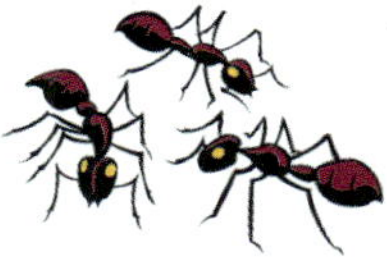
Ants

Butterfly

Praying Mantis

Ladybug

Grasshopper

Insects

Fish

Swimming in Mississippi waters:

Catfish
Flounder
Marlin
Menhaden
Mullet
Red Drum
Red Snapper
Sea Trout
Tuna
White Trout

Sea Critters

OFF THE MISSISSIPPI GULF COAST, YOU MAY FIND:

Clams
Crab
Dolphin
Eel
Jellyfish
Manta Ray
Oyster
Scallops
Shark
Shrimp
Squid
Turtle

Seashells

She sells seashells by the Mississippi seashore!

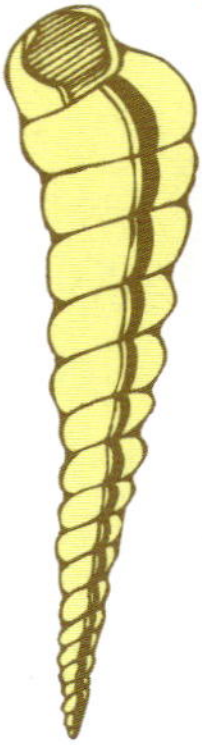

- Auger Shell
- Cerith
- Cockle
- Conch
- Cone shell
- Coquina
- Cowrie
- Helmet Shell
- Janthina
- Moon Shell
- Murex
- Mussel
- Nerite
- Oyster
- Periwinkle
- Slipper Shell
- Wentletrap
- Whelk
- Worm Shell
- Olive Shell

Janthinas travel the ocean upside down! They are supported by a raft of foamy bubbles!

TREEMENDOUS!

THESE TREES GRACE THE STATE OF MISSISSIPPI:

Beech
Dogwood
Hawthorn
Hickory
Magnolia
Oak
Pine
Redbud
Red Maple
Sassafras
Sourwood
Sweetgum
Tulip tree

Wildflowers

Are you crazy about these Mississippi wildflowers?

Black-eyed Susan
Buttercup
Queen Anne's Lace
Firewheel
Goldenrod
Jack-in-the-Pulpit
Lady's Slipper
Chicory
Violet
Cattail
Lupine

Cream of the Crops

Mississippi's agricultural products include:

Pecans

Yams
(sweet potatoes)

Cotton

Hogs

Wheat

Corn

Peanuts

Hay

Peaches

Soybeans

Dairy Cattle

Chickens

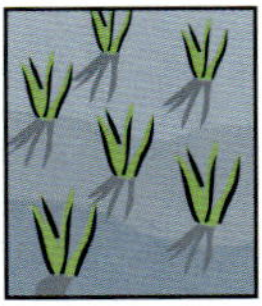
Rice

Watermelon

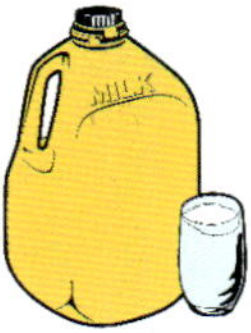
Milk

Trivia

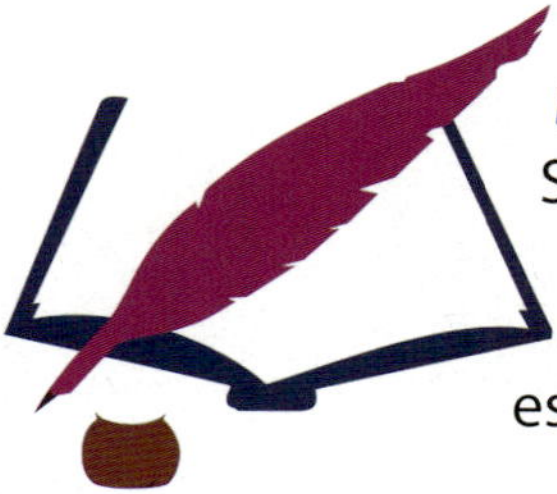

1871–*FIRST LAND-GRANT COLLEGE* in the United States for African-Americans (now Alcorn State University) established

1909–Mississippi becomes first state to have a *PARENT-TEACHER ASSOCIATION (PTA)*

1935–"King of Rock 'n Roll" born in Tupelo; *ELVIS PRESLEY* grew up to sell more than one billion records

1907— *THE 4-H CLUB* was founded in Holmes County

LARGEST Mississippi city–Jackson

Festivals

Mardi Gras, Pascagoula and Natchez–held in February

Natchez Trace Festival, Kosciusko–held in April

Civil War Reenactment, Vicksburg–held in May

Shrimp Festival, Biloxi–held in May; includes the crowning of a queen and the blessing of the shrimp fleet

Watermelon Festival, Mize–held in July

Delta Blues Festival, Greenville–held in September

Mississippi State Fair, Jackson–held the second week of October

Trees of Christmas Festival, Meridian–held in December

Calendar

Martin Luther King, Jr. Day, *3rd Monday in January*

Presidents' Day, *3rd Monday in February*

Confederate Memorial Day, *April 25*

Memorial Day, *Last Monday in May*

Independence Day, *July 4*

Columbus Day, *2nd Monday in October*

Veterans Day, *November 11*

Thanksgiving, *the 4th Thursday in November*

Christmas, *December 25*

Famous Food

Mississippi is famous for the following delicious foods!

- Fried catfish
- Mutton
- Bread pudding with rum sauce
- Banana caramel pie
- Mississippi Mud Pie
- Shrimp
- Tomato sandwiches
- Grits
- Pecan pie
- Rice

Industry

Mississippi Works!

At least 125 Fortune 500 companies have built factories, warehouses, or national headquarters in Mississippi.

The transportation industry is Mississippi's largest employer. Other important industries include: milling lumber, crafting hardwoods, furniture making, food processing, and making machinery.

Other major employers in the state include: clothing manufacturers, paper mills, pharmaceutical manufacturers, and firms which make surgical appliances and supplies.

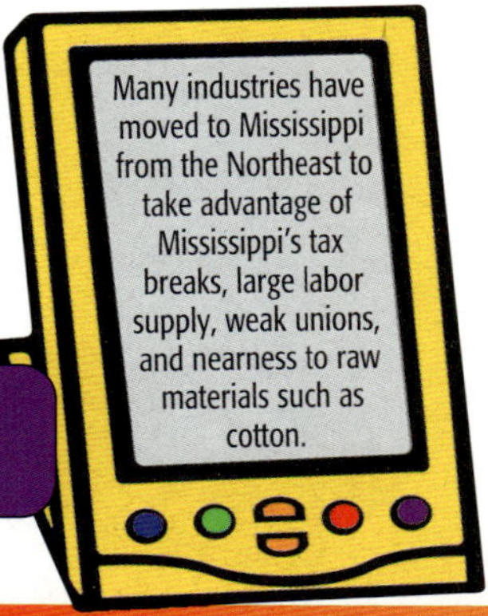

State Books & Websites

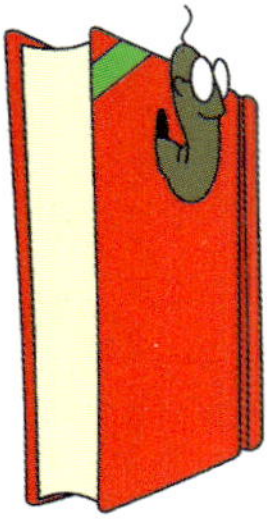

My First Book about Mississippi by Carole Marsh

America the Beautiful: Mississippi by Charles and Linda George

From Sea to Shining Sea: Mississippi by Dennis Fradin

Let's Discover the States: Mississippi by the Aylesworths

Mississippi

Words to Know

GLOSSARY WORDS

abolitionist: a person opposed to slavery

blues: a type of folk music with a slow tempo and sad words; first developed by African-Americans

civil rights: the rights of all citizens regardless of race, religion, gender, etc. to vote, to enjoy life, liberty, property, and equal protection under the law

constitution: a document outlining the role of a government

emancipation: to be set free

picayune: of little value; small

protest: to speak out against; object

raconteur: person who is skilled in telling stories

rogue: a dishonest person; scoundrel

secede: to voluntarily give up being a part of an organized group

valor: boldness in facing danger

Mississippi Spelling Bee

Here are some Mississippi-related words to learn! To take the Spelling Bee, have someone call out the words and you spell them aloud or write them on a piece of paper.

Spelling Words

alluvial	plantation
bayou	Pushmataha
Biloxi	Reconstruction
Chickasaw	secession
metropolitan	segregation
Mississippi	Tallahatchie
Natchez	Tombigbee
Ojibwa	Tupelo
Pascagoula	Yazoo
Pemberton	

ABOUT THE AUTHOR...

CAROLE MARSH has been writing about Mississippi for more than 20 years. She is the author of the popular Mississippi State Stuff series for young readers and creator, along with her son, Michael Marsh, of "Mississippi Facts and Factivities," a CD-ROM widely used in Mississippi schools. The author of more than 100 Mississippi books and other supplementary educational materials on the state, Marsh is currently working on a new collection of Mississippi materials for young people. Marsh correlates her Mississippi materials to the Mississippi Social Studies Framework. Many of her books and other materials have been inspired by or requested by Mississippi teachers and librarians.

EDITORIAL ASSISTANTS:

Billie Walburn

Terry Briggs

Jill Sanders